SQL

*Comprehensive Beginner's
Guide for Newbies*

Introduction

If you strive to successfully learn SQL, reading this introduction to our book is your first step. SQL can be thought of as a complicated subject when it doesn't have to be. This book will provide you with a thorough overview of all that SQL entails. You will learn the basic terms that are associated with the relational database language. Provided will also be basic commands that you can start out using. You will also be provided with a step by step process on how to set up and manage your first database table.

A lot of people wonder what the point is in taking the time to learn SQL. There are many benefits that SQL brings to your life and career most importantly. For business, it is an invaluable tool that employers strive for their employees to acquire. If you are pursuing a successful career in business, SQL can be very beneficial for not only you, but any future or present employer lucky enough to have you. The basic and advanced knowledge of SQL will easily give you the upper hand when working with relational databases and inquiring about any and every type of data feedback.

If you strive to be independent in the career world of business, SQL is a step in the right direction towards being self-sufficient and can give you the potential to make almost **twice as much** as the average household income in the US. The statistics involved in those who make use of SQL are simply extraordinary. It may seem complicated but it is more than worth the time and energy to make use of it.

SQL can be simple in the fact that it is similar to the English language. It requires structure just as any language does. There are basic rules to follow when using any syntax which would be the equivalent to a sentence. It is a simple thing to learn, it just involves endless possibilities and syntaxes that need to be memorized. Over time, it will be simpler to remember syntaxes when you practice the use of them.

Additionally, if you want to master Computer Programming, we have guides on **Python and JavaScript**. And for anyone interested in surfing the Internet anonymously, we have books on **TOR and Anonymous Internet Surfing.** And finally, no savvy computer user's arsenal would be complete without a basic understanding of **Hacking** (don't worry it's the good kind); so we have books on that fascinating topic as well!!

Check out our Amazon author page to find resources such as this- AND MORE:

https://www.amazon.com/HACKING-Beginner-Penetration-Security-Programming-ebook/dp/B01N8ZF5F4

https://www.amazon.com/PYTHON-Beginner-Practical-Programming-Beginners-ebook/dp/B01N91WKHD

If you check out our Programming Library, you WILL increase your earning capacity and marketability at any company dramatically. You will confidently walk into any interview knowing that your skill sets **will be valued** and you have something unique to bring to the table. So don't miss out!!

If you are ready to take a successful step towards a better career and financial independence, keep reading the following pages and you will become closer to achieving your business goals.

So let's get started. It's time to master SQL.

Table of Contents

Chapter 1:
Why Learn SQL?

As mentioned briefly in the introduction, there are many benefits to reap when you successfully and thoroughly learn SQL. This is a short chapter that focuses in detail and more specifically on the benefits and reasons to take into consideration in order to motivate you to take your time and put forth dedication in learning SQL. It can be one of the best career decisions you can make for your life. By being able to rely on your own knowledge of SQL instead of leaning on someone else for information, it is guaranteed to provide you with a whole slew of advantages. Learning SQL will also allow you to do much more than you would have been able to do without the use of it. SQL is the main and primary language used in working with data in a relational database management system or (RDBMS). Listed below are five great reasons to consider before vaguely learning SQL. You should want to be able to attain a vast knowledge of SQL in the future once you are done with this chapter.

SQL Gives You a High Potential to Make Great Money

SQL gives you the opportunity to make a lot more extra money. SQL developers can earn an average of $92,000 a year. SQL database administrators or (DBA's) can make an average of around $97,000 a year. Both of these salaries are twice as much as the average income per household in the US. Learning SQL can be a very easy way to make much more money than what you might make right now.

Employers Want Individuals with SQL Skills

An individual that has a thorough knowledge of SQL brings many advantages to any employer, especially those involved in business. Not only will it benefit your employer, it will also benefit you. You will be much more employable when walking into an interview. After you get the job, you will be much more likely to be offered a higher salary than what you might have been offered without the skill of knowing SQL. SQL not only makes you more likely to be offered a job and a higher paying job, it also opens up more business and career opportunities for you in your career path.

Get Any and Every Question Answered Your Way

When it comes to your yearly sales or ratings, SQL can answer any of the questions you may have about your business or any data in your database. This allows you to be self-sufficient and more independent in the business world. This keeps you from having to ask questions or rely on the knowledge of others or going to other sources in order to get the information that you need. Suppose you are an employer and you want to save costs of using someone with the knowledge of SQL. Maybe you are a business owner that strives to be successful in the future. The knowledge of SQL may be essential for obtaining more success in your business. SQL can help you take one more step to helping your business take off on full-throttle.

No More Crashes in Excel

Millions and even billions of rows of data are able to be stored in relational database systems. When you attempt to move large amounts of this data into programs like Excel, it can be too much and cause a crash. A crash will cause you to start all over and re-track your steps. This will end not only making things more complicated but it will end up wasting much of your valuable time.

When you know how to make use of SQL, you are able to use programs that can withstand however much data is needed to be stored. These programs will ensure that no crashes will occur and will save your time and efforts in tasks that don't necessarily require too much of a process.

You Won't Have to Wonder How You Made a Report

Queries in SQL can be easily saved and re-used whenever you want to double check something. Programs like Excel are unable to save any processes you used in order to obtain your data. SQL codes on the other hand only need to be written once and saved. After that, you are able to open and run any processes that you used in your report. This is just another way that SQL can make your life a lot simpler and take up less time than what other programs might do.

So although SQL may be associated as a complicated and timely subject to learn, it is worth any of the efforts that you put forth in order to learn this language of databases. In fact, it is simple and will save you mass amounts of time in the future. Not only will it save time, it will save money as well. Whether it's saving you money or making you money, it is quite worthy of your time especially if you are pursuing a career in business or pursuing your own business. SQL can be an essential part of knowledge that you need in order to be successful in your career path. It can not only open doors for your career path but also make you a great asset to any employer. Taking your time now to save time and gain more money for yourself or your business is all worth it. If you are ready to learn the basics of SQL, continue reading on to the next chapter and see what is in store for your mind.

Chapter 2:
Basics of SQL

Before you dive into the processes that SQL contains, it is important that you understand the basics associated with learning this complex language of databases. First off, it is important to know what SQL stands for, which is Standard Query Language. This language is used in order to communicate between databases about different data types and in order to manage those databases. There are various different data types that can be stored in a database. These data types are stored in tables which are formed by columns and rows just how Excel is formatted. Columns can be referred to as fields. Listed below is a basic list of the most basic and common terms used in SQL:

- Database- A collection of tables

- Query- Request for information from a database

- DBMS- Database management system

- RDBMS- Relational database management system

- Table- A set of data that is organized in rows and columns

- Syntax- An arrangement of words and phrases in order to create a statement in SQL.

- Primary Key- This holds a unique value which identifies each record of data in a table. It can be unique or it can be automatically generated.

- Foreign Key- A key field or column that identifies records of data in a table by matching a primary key in a different table

- CRUD- Acronym for the four basic operations of SQL: CREATE, READ, UPDATE, DELETE.

The main difference between DBMS and RDBMS is that RDBMS's store data in a table while DBMS's store data in the form of a file. SQL applies to RDBMS's more than it does with regular DBMS's. The main difference between a primary key and a foreign key is that foreign keys make up primary keys and add complexity to them. Foreign keys in one table can bring up information from data in another table.

It is also important to note that there are three main programs that can be used with SQL. They are MySQL, Access, and Oracle. Some of the commands can vary depending on each program. Any differences in the uses of the commands will be noted in further chapters. There are many other programs but we will focus mainly on those. If you happen to use a platform that is something other than what is listed, you may want to try some of the other variations of commands shown if one particular command doesn't bring the promised outcome.

Data Types

As mentioned beforehand, there are various types of data that can be stored in databases. Listed below are some of the data types that can be found and used in a database:

- Byte- allows numbers from the range of 0-255 to be contained. Storage is 1 byte.

- Currency- this holds 15 whole dollar digits with additional decimal places up to 4. Storage is 8 bytes.

- Date/Time- will be used for dates and times. Storage is 8 bytes.

- Double- This is a double precision floating-point which will handle most decimals. Storage is 8 bytes.

- Integer- This will allow of the amounts between -32,768 and 32,767. Storage is 2 bytes.

- Text- This is used for combinations of texts and numbers. This can up to 255 characters to be stored.

- Memo- This can be used for text of larger amounts. It can store 65,536 characters. Memo fields can't be sorted but they can be searched.

- Long- This will allow between -2,147,483,648 and 2,147,483,647 whole numbers. Storage is 4 bytes.

- Single- This is a single precision floating-point that will handle most decimals. Storage is 4 bytes.

- AutoNumber- This field can automatically give each record of data its own number which usually starts out at 1. Storage is 4 bytes.

- Yes/No- This is a logical field that can be displayed as yes/no, true/false, or on/off. The use of true and false should be equivalent to -1 and 0. In these fields, null values are not allowed. Storage is 1 bit.

- Ole Object- This can store BLOBS such as pictures, audio, video. BLOBs are which Binary Large Objects. The storage is 1 gigabyte (GB).

- Hyperlink- This contains links to other files like web pages.

- Lookup Wizard- This will let you make an options list. A drop down list will then allow it to be chosen. Storage is 4 bytes.

Overall, data types can be categorized into three different types of data. They are either

1. Character types

2. Number types

3. Date/Time types

Character types consist of text. Number contain amounts or numbers. Date/Time types consist of a recorded date or time. Listed below are some of the types of data of each category.

Character Data Types

- CHAR(size)- A fixed length string can be held with this data type. It is able to hold special characters, letters and numbers. This can store up to 255 characters.

- VARCHAR(size)- This can hold a variable string length which is able to hold special characters, letters and numbers. The size will be specified in parenthesis. It can store up to 255 characters. This will automatically be a text type that it is converted to if the value is placed higher than 255 characters.

- TINYTEXT- This holds a string with 255 characters of maximum length.

- TEXT- This holds a string with 65,535 characters of maximum length.

- MEDIUMTEXT- This holds a string with 16,777,215 of maximum characters.

- LONGTEXT- This holds a string with 4,294,967,295 of maximum characters.

- BLOB- These hold 65,535 bytes of maximum data.

- MEDIUMBLOB- These hold 16,777,215 bytes of maximum data.

- LONGBLOB- These hold 4,294,967,295 bytes of maximum data.

- ENUM(x,y,z, etc.)- A list that contains possible values. This list can hold 65535 max values. When a value is entered into the list that isn't contained inside that list, a blank value will be entered instead. The order that the values are entered is how they will also be sorted.

- SET- This is similar to the ENUM data type. This data type holds a maximum of 64 list items and is able to store more than one choice.

Number Data Types

The most common of the options are listed below along with their storage type when it comes to bytes and values:

- TINYINT(size)- Holds -128 to 127, or 0 to 255 unsigned.

- SMALLINT(size)- Holds -32768 to 32767, or 0 to 65535 unsigned.

- MEDIUMINT(size)- Holds -8388608 to 8388607, or 16,777,215 unsigned.

- INT(size)- Holds -2,147,483,648 to 2,147,483,647, or 4,294,967,295 unsigned.

- BIGINT(size)- Holds 9,223,372,036,854,775,808 to 9,223,372,036,854,775,807 or 18,446,744,073,709,551,615 unsigned.

- FLOAT(size,d)- This is a tiny number with a decimal point that can float. Specified in the size parameter is the maximum amount of digits. Specified in the d parameter is the maximum amount of digits in the right of the decimal point.

- DOUBLE(size,d)- This is a large number with a decimal point that floats. The maximum number of digits may be specified in the size parameter (size). The maximum number of digits to the right of the decimal point is specified in the d parameter (d).

- DECIMAL(size,d)- This type is string that is stored which allows a decimal point that is fixed. The maximum number of digits may be specified in the size parameter (size). Specified in the d parameter is the maximum amount of digits to the right of the decimal point.

- An extra option is found in integer types that is called unsigned. Normally, an integer will go from a value of negative to positive. When adding the unsigned attribute will be able to move the range up higher so that it will not start at a negative number, but a zero. That is why the unsigned option is mentioned after the specified numbers listed for the different data types.

Date/Time Data Types

The options for date are:

- DATE()- This is in order to enter a date in the format of YYYY-MM-DD as in 2016-04-19 (April 19th, 2016)

- DATETIME()- This is in order to enter a combination of date and time in the format of YYYY-MM-DD and HH:MM:SS as in 13:30:26 (1:30 p.m. at 26 seconds)

- TIMESTAMP()- This is in order to enter to store the number of seconds and match the current time zone. The format is YYYY-MM-DD HH:MM:SS.

- TIME()- This will allow you to enter the time. The format is HH:MM:SS.

- YEAR()- This is in order to enter a year in a two or four digit format. A four-digit format would be as 2016 or 1992. A two digit format would be as 72 or 13.

It is important to note that if the DATETIME and TIMESTAMP will return to the same format. When compared to each other, they will still work in different ways. The TIMESTAMP will automatically update to the current time and date of the time zone present TIMESTAMP will also accept other various formats available such as YYYYMMDDHHMMSS, YYMMDDHHMMSS, YYYYMMDD, and also YYMMDD.

CRUD: CREATE, READ, UPDATE and DELETE

CRUD is the acronym as mentioned before that states the four basic commands of SQL. This is a great place for anyone to start out that is trying to learn and understand how SQL works. It clearly and simply shows the basics in SQL and how to adequately use SQL in RDBMS. Listed below are the four commands and what they are used for.

- Create- The command used in order to fill out data into tables.

- Read- The command used in order to query or read data that is contained in a table.

- Update- The command used in order to change or manipulate data that is already in a table.

- Delete- The command used in order to remove data from a table.

After you master the use of these commands, you can move on to other commands with a better understanding of how each syntax works in a database. Later on in this book, you will be presented with basic commands to use in SQL that will cover the CRUD commands. As mentioned before, SQL is similar to the English language. The English language commands structure and has basic rules to follow. Listed below is a basic list to keep in mind when putting any command into a database. These rules will allow you to keep from making common mistakes or experiencing snags.

SQL Rules:

- The names of tables and columns should always start with a letter.

- After all the column names are properly started, numbers, letters and even underscores can be included in the rest of the column name.

- A column name can have a maximum amount of 30 characters of text in length.

- You can't use keywords such as 'select', 'create', or 'insert'. These keywords will confuse the database to thinking you are entering a command.

- Every statement in SQL should end with a ';' just how every English sentence ends with a period.

Creating Data

In order to create or add data, you first need to be able to create a table in the database. In order to create a new table, 'CREATE TABLE' is the statement to be entered into the database. You should first place the words 'CREATE TABLE'. Then, a table name should be entered. Open parenthesis should be followed by the keywords. The column name and data type should be followed by closed parenthesis where additional parameters are defined. The syntax for this command should be formed as shown below:

CREATE TABLE table_name
(column_1 data_type,
column_2 data_type,
column_3 data_type);

Reading Data

You can query the data and be able to see what is stored in each table after the data is already saved into the database. You can also filter and sort the data in three different ways. Listsed below are the three statements that are highly important when querying your data into the database:

• SELECT
• FROM
• WHERE

The SELECT statement will tell the computer that you want values returned back to you and what those values are.

The FROM statement will tell you what values can be found by showing you what tables are available in the database.

The WHERE statement will list the conditions that need certain information to be meet before it can be chosen. Until you move past the two basics, this statement can't be used.

Update Data

You can make any changes to any data in a column and in any row after you initially enter the data. The 'UPDATE' statement can be used in order to update or change any records. The UPDATE statement can be used with the WHERE clause. Using clauses in your SQL commands should be used accurately and precisely. For instance, if the WHERE clause is misplaced in the command or left out, all the information in the table will be updated.

Deleting Data

When data becomes obsolete in a database, you need to remove the data. You are able to either delete complete tables altogether or just a few rows from tables. Just as the same rule that applies to the 'UPDATE' statement when it comes to the importance of the 'WHERE' clause, it has the same kind of importance with the 'DELETE' statement. If the 'WHERE' clause is not properly placed or is left out of the format, all of the rows and data will end up being deleted. In the instance that you want to clean up your database and some of the tables that it contains, or even all its rows, the 'DROP TABLE' statement can be used. The 'DELETE' statement is different from this statement. The 'DELETE' statement can delete all data that is contained in a table. This will leave the table by itself and its defined structure. When the statement 'DROP TABLE' is used, it will remove the table and all of the rows and data contained in it.

Chapter 3:
Managing Your First Table

Now that you are more familiar with how SQL works and some of the basic terms and how commands are formed, it's time to put those to use. No matter what your reasons are for using SQL, you will be able to learn how to successfully complete your first table and apply the CRUD commands to it along with other commands.

Create Table

The first step would obviously be that you need to create a table in order to manage or do anything with it. Whether you want to start out with something more specific that you could really use later on, or just something to get you started, you want to decide what to make your table about. Once you have decided on your table topic, you will want to consider how many rows you will need and what data types your table will need to hold. Below is the syntax to use in order to create your table.

CREATE TABLE "table_name"
("column1" "data type"
"column2" "data type"
"column3" "data type");

It doesn't matter if you use all uppercase or lowercase words. The result will be the same. It is easier to identify the command you are using though whenever you put it in all uppercase letters. Of course, you could use this exact syntax and get a very basic table. But to be more specific and to understand how your table will turn out, you want to name your table according to whatever you decide to use it for. An easy topic to start off with is "Clients" or "Orders" since you will most likely use SQL for the business world. The three columns could be used to collect the clients' first name, last name, and address. If you were to follow that example, you would insert the name of the column in the column1, column2, and column3 area. Remember the data types that were listed earlier? That's where those come into use. They may seem like information overload but they are actually quite simple to use once you start to incorporate them into your tables. You can see how they are put to use in the example shown below.

CREATE TABLE Clients
(first name varchar (15),
last name varchar (20),
address varchar (30));

This would result in a table named "Clients" with three columns to contain their first and last name and their address. The name doesn't have to be included. You could simply leave it as first and last without the name following it. The example is just to be more specific and clear. The number in parenthesis dictates how many characters can be held in that column. Remember how the data types had the word size in parenthesis next to the name? That's where this comes to use and you can decide how many characters you want held in the column. Although you need to keep in mind that each data type has a storage limit. The storage limit for varchar data types is 255 characters. Varchar data type will allow you to enter either text or numbers into the column. Char will allow you to just enter text. Varchar will give you more options for whatever you need to enter into your column. This is useful for the address column as those contain both text and numbers. If you wanted to include a column in your chart that was for their age, this data type would only need to include numbers. You would use the number data type. It would be included into your table as shown below.

CREATE TABLE Clients
(first varchar(15),
last varchar(20),
address varchar(30),
age number(2));

This means your table would include a total of four columns and the age column would only be able to include numbers up to 2 digits. It is also important to note that after the original command of CREATE TABLE along with the name of the table beside it, that what is included in the table is defined by the parenthesis. It starts and ends with parenthesis with ';' to end the command. Even though the number of the data type is defined in parenthesis, you still need to add on an extra with a following ';' in order to complete the command. The parenthesis for the numbers are different than the parenthesis that define the command details.

Read Data

Now that you have successfully created your first table, the second step in using this information is to be able to query or read it. It was mentioned earlier that in this step, three basic clauses can be used in order to filter what information you want to receive back to you. The three main clauses are:

- SELECT

- FROM

- WHERE

In order to use the SELECT command to query your data back from you, you can select your table name. This will bring up the whole table that you just created. The syntax would be formatted as shown below.

SELECT * FROM table_name

If you wanted to select specific columns from your table or just one column, the following syntax would be used as shown below.

SELECT column1,
(FROM table_name);

Without specifically using the FROM clause, you will not be able to bring up your data.

If you wanted to be more specific on what kind of data you request back to you, you can use the WHERE clause. This clause uses different operator values in order to filter what information comes back. Below is a list of operators that can be used in order to filter what is returned to you.

- '='- equal to

- ' >'- greater than

- ' <'- less than

- ' >='- greater than or equal to

- ' <='- less than or equal to

- '<> '- not equal to

- '%'- can either appear before or after specific characters or can match and possible character

- 'BETWEEN'- between two values

- 'LIKE'- to search for a pattern, this can be used

- 'IN'- multiple values of possibilities in a column

These operators would be placed in the syntax as shown below.

SELECT column1, column2, column3,
(FROM table_name
WHERE column_name operator value);

We will go more into the specifics of using these operators later on. Right now it is just important that you know what kind of operators can be placed when using the WHERE clause.

The ORDER BY clause can also be used when querying data. You can use this clause to manage how the information retrieved is arranged.

Update Data

The next step in understanding how to use SQL for your tables is to be able to update data in your table. All data will have to be updated somehow sooner or later. This occurs on a daily basis for larger businesses. The WHERE clause can also be used in the UPDATE command. It is very important where the WHERE clause is placed. If you do not specify the clause or you misplace it, all the information will be updated without the clause or the wrong information will be updated.

UPDATE table_name
(SET column_name = new value
WHERE column_name operator value);

There are many different ways that data can be updated in your table. One of the most simplest syntaxes to use is shown below. This can be used to basically update any values held in your table.

UPDATE table_name
(SET column_name=value);

Delete Data

After you have mastered creating, reading, and updating data, the last command you should learn is how to delete data when it becomes obsolete. The most basic syntax you can use in order to delete data in a table is shown below.

DELETE FROM table_name
WHERE column_name operator value;

The operator value can give you more options when choosing different data to delete. If you wanted to just delete a certain column, you would simply remove the operator value and use the syntax shown below.

DELETE FROM table_name
(WHERE column_name);

There are other commands such as the DROP TABLE command that you can use in order to delete necessary data. The other commands will be presented later on.

When it comes to the commands of SQL, they can be categorized into these four categories of commands or "CRUD". Being able to understand and use SQL is much more than these four commands though. There is much more that SQL commands have to offer. From basic to advanced commands, there are plenty of commands to offer specific and unique results for whatever you are trying to achieve whether it be business related or in order for you to successfully understand SQL.

Chapter 4:
Basic SQL Commands

Listed in this chapter are all of the various commands that you can use in SQL. The more basic commands are at the beginning of the chapter whereas the more advanced commands will be found further on down the chapter. The command name will be listed along with how it can be used and how to properly use it with the syntax included. Operators and clauses along with keywords will be mentioned after the basic commands. Examples will be shown on how to properly use each command.

Commands

CREATE DATABASE

In order to create your own database, you would use the following syntax as shown below.

CREATE DATABASE database_name

CREATE TABLE

After you create your database, you want to start creating tables to be entered into the database as well.

The CREATE TABLE command can be used as shown below.

CREATE TABLE table_name
(column_name1 data_type,
column_name2 data_type,
column_name3 data_type,);

Here is an example:

CREATE TABLE Individuals
(Id number(20),
Last varchar (255)
First varchar (255)
Address varchar (255)
City varchar (255));

The result would give you a table of Individuals with their information sorted out by their first and last name, their address, and the city that they are located in. The Id at the top stands for their ID number that would be entered in as a number. The ID column is able to hold a number of up to 20 digits.

INSERT

After you have your database and your tables all set up, you may find yourself needing to add another row into an existing table. In order to do this without setting up a completely new table, you can use the INSERT INTO command. The syntax is as shown below.

INSERT INTO table_name
VALUES (value1, value2, value3);

The following syntax will only be specific to the values of a column. It won't be able to specify any of the column names. In the instance that you want to specify the column values along with their names as well, you can use the following syntax as shown below.

INSERT INTO table_name
(column_1, column_2, column_3)
VALUES (value1, value2, value3)

If you wanted to be able to insert a new row into the table, it would be done using a similar syntax as shown below.

INSERT INTO table_name
VALUES ('insert various row information here')
example: (3 such as 'row 3', 'Williams such as last name', 'Travis such as first name')

This will allow you to be able to insert multiple amounts of various data into different rows at the same time.

To be able to insert data into specific columns, you can use the following syntax shown below.

INSERT INTO Individuals
(Id, Last, First)
VALUES (5 , 'Thompson', 'Jessica')

This would enter the information into row 5 and the column of the last name the name "Thompson" would be entered. Then the following name "Jessica" would be entered into the first name column.

Now that we have thoroughly covered the first few basic commands associated with the CREATE type commands of CRUD, it's now time to move on to the next type of commands of the acronym. The next step would be to query or read your data that you have created and inserted into your database. The next command will show you how to easily and specifically retrieve information from your database.

SELECT

In order to be able to query and read data in your database, you want to be able to select whatever data you want to be retrieved back to you. This is where the SELECT command comes into use. The command can be formed as shown in the syntax shown below.

SELECT columns
FROM tables
[JOIN joins]
WHERE search_condition]
[GROUP BY grouping_columns]
[HAVING search_condition]
[ORDER BY sort_columns];

This is a more complex syntax that can be used for a very specific search. The operators, clauses and keywords mentioned in the syntax will be introduced after the basic commands are presented. This is a syntax that you can come back to once you thoroughly understand how to use each part.

In order to retrieve a single column from a table, the following syntax can be used as shown below.

SELECT column
FROM table;

In order to retrieve multiple columns from a table, use the following syntax shown below.

SELECT columns
FROM table;

In order to retrieve all columns from a table, you are selecting the table as a whole since you are not wanting one or more columns over the others. In order to select a table, the keyword "FROM" comes into use. Use the following syntax as shown below.

SELECT * FROM table;

Just how we selected multiple columns from a table earlier, the same is applied as shown below. For instance, say you have a table named "Clients" and you want to search your clients by their first and last name. You would use the syntax as shown below.

SELECT Last, First
FROM Clients

Here is another example of how you would use the SELECT command to pull up a whole table instead of specified columns of a table. Let's say you just wanted to search your client list how it is in the database without searching clients by their first or last name. You would use the syntax shown below.

SELECT * FROM Clients

Now that we have covered the create and read type commands, the next commands will be update as a part of the CRUD commands. Now that you understand how to create and read the data that you enter into your database and tables, the next step that you will need to do is to be able to update the data that you've entered.

UPDATE

When you need to update data that exists in a table, you can use the UPDATE command in order to do so. It can be used as shown in the syntax below.

UPDATE table_name
SET column1=value, column2=value,
column3=value
[WHERE search_condition];

Without properly placing the WHERE clause, all of the data or the improper data will be updated by the command. Listed below is another way to properly use the WHERE clause in the UPDATE command as an example of a specific table with specific data.

UPDATE Clients
(SET First= 'Jason'
City= 'Rochester'
WHERE Last= 'Knight');

This example would add in the first name and city that the client lives in by searching for his last name. Of course, you can be more specific with the WHERE clause as you might have plenty of clients in a chart with the same last name. You could use the WHERE clause to search for other conditions in a table to make sure your results will be specific and sure.

Now that you understand how to not only create and read data in a database but now you understand how to update it as well. The last step of "CRUD" is delete. There are several more ways to delete information in SQL than you would think. The following commands listed will be different ways that you can delete data to your own needs or preference.

DELETE

When you find yourself needing to delete rows in a table, the DELETE command can be used in order to do so. To properly use it, follow the syntax shown below.

DELETE FROM table_name
[WHERE search_condition];

Here, the search condition would be used to fill in the name or placement of the row. If the WHERE clause is improperly used with the DELETE command, all of the records will be deleted as a result.

When you want to be able to remove just one individual row from your table, you can use the following syntax example as shown below.

DELETE FROM Clients
WHERE Last= 'Johnson'
AND First= 'Sarah';

Here, the AND keyword is used as well as the WHERE clause. The AND keyword will be presented more in depth later on. Here, you can see that it is used to add a more specific search to aid the deletion process of an individual in the

Clients table. The example would simply and only remove that one client with that first and last name. If you had other clients with the same name, this is where more specific identification can be used such as a unique ID number for your clients in your database.

In the case that you want to be able to delete all the rows in a table, you can use the following syntax as shown below.

DELETE * FROM table_name;

DROP

The DROP command can be used in order to delete an index that is contained in a table. The DROP command can also be used to delete a database or a table. Indexes can be created in order to speed up a search in your database by making your tables more defined. They won't be visible to those who view the table, only those who search for the table. Shown below is a syntax on how to properly use the DROP command when deleting an index. There are four variations for the syntax depending on what platform you are using SQL on.

Access:

DROP INDEX index_name

MS SQL Server:

DROP INDEX
table_name.index_name

Oracle:

DROP INDEX index_name

MySQL:

ALTER TABLE table_name
DROP INDEX index_name

When you want to be able to delete a table in your database, you can use the DROP TABLE command in order to do so. The syntax is properly shown below.

How to use the DROP TABLE command:

DROP TABLE table_name

When you want to be able to delete the whole database itself, you can use the DROP DATABASE command in order to do so. The proper syntax is shown below.

How to use the DROP DATABASE command:

DROP DATABASE database_name

TRUNCATE

The TRUNCATE command can be used whenever you want to delete data that is already contained in a table without removing the whole table itself. This can be useful for times when you want to start fresh without completely start over in your table. In order to properly use the TRUNCATE command, the syntax is shown below.

TRUNCATE TABLE table_name

That then completes the four categories of commands that "CRUD" stands for. The following syntaxes will be of operators, clauses and keywords that can be used in commands. Some of them have already been shown in the commands listed. These extras can add precise work to your commands and be quite useful.

Operators and Clauses

AND

When you want to look a client or anything in your table, you can use the AND operator to make the search more specific. If you were looking up a client, this could be used to look the individual up by their first AND last name. If you were looking for a Garrett Lee in your database, you would use the following syntax in order to use the AND operator to do so.

SELECT * FROM Clients
WHERE First= 'Garrett'
AND Last= 'Lee'

OR

This operator is similar to the AND operator. If you wanted to be able to find two different kinds of clients in your database by their first OR last name, you could use the following syntax as shown below.

SELECT * FROM Clients
WHERE First= 'John'
OR Last= 'Thomas'

This would be able to bring up any client in your database with either the first name of John or the last name of Thomas. Of course, you could use this operator in whatever way you wanted to in order to bring up more precise results.

AND/OR

This operator can be used in order to filter your records using more than one condition. The AND and OR operators can be quite useful by themselves but they become even more useful when combined together in order to refine your search. The AND operator will display two records due to the two specific conditions if the data search applies to both. When a record is adequate to either the first or second condition, the OR operator will display the more specific results. The syntax is example is shown below.

SELECT * FROM Clients
WHERE Last= 'Jones'
AND (First= 'Carl' OR First= 'Mark')

By combining these commands together, the results will select individuals that have the same last name that is specified. This will pick up on individuals that have the last name that is equal to the last name "Jones" and the first names of either "Carl" or "Mark".

NOT

This operator can be used in order to rule by one condition when searching your database. This operator is used as a clause with the SELECT command. The proper syntax is shown below.

SELECT * First, Last, State
FROM Clients
WHERE NOT (State = 'AK');

The results would bring up clients by their first and last name along with the state that they lived in. It would bring up all clients except for the ones that live in Alaska. Of course, you could add more states than just one for your search.

WHERE

The WHERE clause has been shown in previous commands in order to be specific to the use of the command. It is very important where you place the WHERE clause. In order to make sure you have a good idea of how to properly use it, included below are two syntaxes that are shown in correct and incorrect formats along with the initial syntax that should be used.

```
SELECT column_names
FROM table_name
WHERE test_column operator value;
```

Say you want to retrieve clients from a city:

```
SELECT * FROM Clients
WHERE City= 'Portland'
```

How to use WHERE clause with text and numeric values:

Correct:

```
SELECT * FROM Clients
[WHERE First='Amanda']
```

Incorrect:

```
SELECT * FROM Clients
(WHERE First=Amanda)
```

Correct:

```
SELECT * FROM Clients
WHERE Year=1985
```

Incorrect:

SELECT * FROM Clients
WHERE Year= '1985'

GROUP BY

This operator can be used with other commands in order to group the result of one or more columns of a table. The proper syntax use is shown below.

SELECT column_name
Aggregate_function (column_name)
FROM table_name
WHERE column_name operator value
GROUP BY column_name

This operator can also be used in order to find the total sum that a client has purchased from you in the case that you are a business owner that keeps your records in your database. A proper syntax in order to use this is shown below.

SELECT Clients, SUM (Orders Purchased)
FROM Products
GROUP BY Clients

This would bring up how much an individual had purchased from you by pulling up the orders that had been purchased from the products.

In order to bring up more than one column, you can use the syntax example below:

SELECT Clients, Date, SUM (Orders Purchased)
FROM Products
GROUP BY Clients, Date

This would bring up a column for each of the sums according to the clients and the date as well.

Keywords

ORDER BY

Similar to the GROUP BY operator, the ORDER BY keyword is not much different. It will pull up your results in a specific order depending on what you decide to put in for your benefit. By default, your data that you retrieve will come back to you in ascending order. In the case that you wanted it to come back in a descending order, you would use the keyword 'DESC'. You can use this keyword in the following syntax example shown below.

SELECT column_names
FROM table_name
ORDER BY sort_columns [ASC | DESC];

In order to sort multiple columns, the following syntax example can be used:

SELECT column_names
FROM table_name
ORDER BY
sort_column1 [ASC | DESC],
sort_column2 [ASC | DESC],
sort_column3 [ASC | DESC];

In order to sort by column positions in relevance:

SELECT column_names
FROM table_name
ORDER BY
sort_number1 [ASC | DESC],
sort_number2 [ASC | DESC],
sort_number3 [ASC | DESC];

In order to sort by order in descending order:

SELECT * FROM Clientss
ORDER BY Last name DESC

The results would bring up data of your clients by their last name from Z to A instead of alphabetical order. In the case of numbers, it would bring up the lowest numbers up to the highest numbers.

DISTINCT

In the event that you need to eliminate any duplicate rows, you can do this by using the DISTINCT keyword to do so. You can use this keyword in the following syntax shown below.

SELECT DISTINCT column_names
FROM table_name

You can also combine the SELECT command with the DISTINCT keyword. If you wanted to be able to find clients from a specific city, you could use the following syntax example shown below.

SELECT DISTINCT New York City
From Clients

This will bring up all the clients in your database that live specifically in New York City.

Chapter 5:
Advanced SQL Commands

Although this is just a beginner's guide, there are plenty of SQL commands that can be quite simple to use. Not only can they be simple, they might even offer plenty of help and simplicity to your searches. Some of you may not have access to an SQL platform while others of you may have access to it every day and are picking up on the skill in order to benefit your employer or your business. Whatever your reasons are for diving into this complex but potentially simple skill, there are other commands available that could be quite useful and simple even if they are considered advanced.

ALIAS

Sometimes you can give a table or column name the use of an alias to the original name when it is too long or complex. Sometimes complicated or long names can end up costing you more time if you are unable to remember the original name. Longer names also present available chances for typos. In order to set up an alias for an existing table or column, the following syntax should be used as shown below.

For tables:

SELECT column_name(s)
FROM table_name
AS alias_name

For columns:

SELECT column_name
AS alias_name
FROM table_name

You can even use an alias for individuals or a row. This can make your results appear less complicated and more clear. Below are two examples of what your results could look like without an alias and how they would look like with one.

How it looks without an alias:

SELECT Shipments.ID,
Clients.Last, Customers.First
FROM Clients, Shipments
WHERE Clients.Last= 'Smith' AND
Clients.First= 'John'

How it looks with an alias:

SELECT po.ID, c.Last, c.First
FROM Clients AS c, Shipments AS po
WHERE p.Last= 'Smith' AND p.First= 'John'

You can see that the Shipments was replaced with the word "po" and clients were changed to "c". For beginners, this might make it a little complicated to read. For business owners with larger volumes of clients, this can shorten what is required of them to read and go over when they are querying data back to them.

ALTER

When you want to be able to add, delete, or modify any columns contained in an existing table, you can use the ALTER TABLE command in order to do so.

In order to add a column to a table:

ALTER TABLE table_name
ADD column_name datatype

In order to delete a column from a table:

ALTER TABLE table_name
DROP COLUMN column_name

You should keep in mind that some databases won't allow a column to be deleted by itself.

In order to change the data type of a column in an existing table:

ALTER TABLE table_name
ALTER COLUMN column_name
Datatype

For this command, if you wanted to be able to add a row into your table, you could use the following syntax example shown below.

ALTER TABLE Clients
ADD Since date

The result will add an empty row to the Clients table and thereafter, you can enter the dates that they have been with you.

In order to change data types:

ALTER TABLE Clients
ALTER COLUMN Since year
datatype

In order to drop a column:

ALTER TABLE Clients
DROP COLUMN Since year

AUTO INCREMENT/ IDENTITY

You can allow a unique number to be created whenever new data is entered into a table. You can do this by using the AUTO INCREMENT command.

The syntax shown below shows an example of the syntax used.

CREATE TABLE Clients
(C_Id int NOT NULL
AUTO_INCREMENT,
Last varchar (255),
First varchar (255),
Address varchar (255),
City varchar (255),
PRIMARY KEY (C_Id));

The example defines the "C_Id" column to be an auto-increment key in the "Clients" table. This will allow the auto-increment feature. By default, the number that it starts out with will be 1 any time that you use the auto-increment feature. With each new entry of data, the total number will increase by 1. This can be used in your table in order to easily keep track of how many clients you have or the specific amount of entries.

In the case that you want the auto-increment feature to start out with another number besides 1, the following syntax example can be used as shown below.

ALTER TABLE Clients
AUTO_INCREMENT=100

This could be useful for specific reasons. Say you are a company that demands a new client that wants to become a member is required to buy a certain amount of products from you before they are a member. Or let's say that a client is buying a membership that costs a set amount. This can be used in order to easily and automatically keep track of how much is accumulated through those accounts.

The AUTO INCREMENT command is not necessary when entering new data into the "Clients" table in order to specify a value for the column.

INSERT INTO Clients (First,Last)
VALUES ('John', 'Smith')

Here is another statement example:

```
CREATE TABLE Clients
(C_Id int PRIMARY KEY IDENTITY,
Last varchar (255) NOT NULL,
First varchar (255),
Address varchar (255),
City varchar (255));
```

The keyword IDENTITY will be used by the server in order for the auto-increment feature to be used. The starting out value will be 1 for the identity keyword and will increased by 1 with every new data entry. To be more specific, in the example, the "C_Id" column will start out at some specified value or increment. You are able to change the identity keyword by using (start, increment).

Using the IDENTITY is not always necessary when inputting a new data entry into the table.

```
INSERT INTO Clients (First,Last)
VALUES ('John', 'Smith')
```

As mentioned before, there are different versions of how to form syntaxes depending on what platform you use for SQL.

Access:

CREATE TABLE Clients
(C_Id PRIMARY KEY AUTOINCREMENT,
Last varchar (255) NOT NULL,
First varchar (255),
Address varchar (255),
City varchar (255));

Again, in the Access database, the default for the increment will be 1 and will increase by 1 with every new data entry. When entering a new record of data into the "Clients" table, it isn't necessary to have a specific value for the "C_Id" column:

INSERT INTO Clients (First,Last)
VALUES ('John', 'Smith')

Oracle:

In the Oracle database system, the auto-increment field will have to be created with the sequence object. This object will generate a number sequence. In order to do this, use the CREATE SEQUENCE command.

CREATE SEQUENCE seq_client
MINVALUE 1
START WITH 1
INCREMENT BY 1
CACHE 10

This will create a sequence that will automatically increase by 1 with each new data entry. In order to specify how many sequence values will be stored in memory and in order to attain faster access, the cache option is placed. In order to enter new data into the "Clients" table, the nextval function will be used to retrieve the next coming value from the seq_client sequence:

INSERT INTO Clients (C_Id,First,Last)
VALUES (seq_client.nextval, 'John', 'Smith')

This statement will insert a new record of data into the "Clients" table. In the example, the next number from the seq_client sequence will be assigned in the "C_Id" column. The "First" column would be set to "John" and the "Last" column would be set to "Smith".

BETWEEN

You are able to select a range of data between two specified values by using the BETWEEN operator. The contained values can be numbers, text, or even dates. You can use the operator in the following syntax shown below.

SELECT column_name(s)
FROM table_name
WHERE column_name
BETWEEN value1 AND value2

If you needed to be able to find data between the months of May and August of a table, you could use this operation. The example of the syntax is shown below.

SELECT * FROM Sales
WHERE Date since
BETWEEN 'May' AND 'August'

This operator could be useful when you want to find the amount of sales you had between two specific dates.

In different databases, the BETWEEN operator can be formed differently.

CREATE INDEX

You can create an index that is contained in tables by using the CREATE INDEX command. Indexes can allow you to find data quickly without having to read an entire table. Any index that you create will not be visible to the user but will be used in order to speed up any searches or queries. When it comes to updating a table that contains an index, it can take more time than what it would take when updating a table without an index. This is because the index also requires to be updated as well. Indexes can be a useful tool for columns and tables that you know will be frequently searched.

In order to create an index:

CREATE INDEX index_name
ON table_name (column_name)

In order to create a unique index:

CREATE UNIQUE INDEX index_name
ON table_name (column_name)

This can vary between the different databases.

IN

Following the WHERE clause, the IN operator can be used in order to allow multiple values to be specified. The operator, along with the WHERE clause should be used in the syntax shown below.

SELECT column_name(s)
FROM table_name
WHERE column_name
IN (value1, value2, value3)

In an example, if you needed to find the values recorded in two different months of your "Clients" table, you would use the statement likewise below:

SELECT * FROM Clients
WHERE Date since IN ('March', 'June')

The result would bring up the two months and the values entered in the "Date since" row.

ISNULL()

This is a function that can be used along with the NVL() and IFNULL() functions. These can be used in order to determine where a value is null or not. When a value is null, it means that it is either invalid, void, or associated with zero.

If you had a table of products that were listed in your inventory and you wanted to figure out which products were out of stock, you could use the ISNULL() function. The following syntax example is shown below.

SELECT ProductName, Price * (InStock + OnOrder)
FROM Products

This wold be able to bring up any quantities listed in the rows of InStock and InOrder of the table. In the example, if any of the values from OnOrder are null, the result will be null. In order to specify how you will want to treat any null values, Microsoft's function of ISNULL(), can be used. For other databases, the NVL() and IFNULL() can achieve the same result when used.

Access:

SELECT ProductName, Price * (InStock + ISNULL(OnOrder,0))
FROM Products

Oracle:

Oracle database does not have the ISNULL() function but the NVL() function can be used in order to achieve the same result that would be found in other databases.

SELECT ProductName, Price * (InStock + NVL(OnOrder,0))
FROM Products

MySQL:

This database also does not have the ISNULL() function. To achieve the same result, the IFNULL() function can be used instead.

SELECT ProductName, Price * (InStock + IFNULL(OnOrder,0))
FROM Products

LIKE

When you need to search for a specified pattern that appears in a column, you can use the LIKE operator along with the WHERE clause in order to do so. The proper syntax is shown below.

SELECT column_name(s)
FROM table_name
WHERE column_name
LIKE pattern

In an example, if you have a client chart and you need to find the individuals that live in a city that starts with a specific letter, the LIKE operator can be applied as shown below:

SELECT * FROM Clients
WHERE City LIKE 'd%'

The result would bring up the cities in the clients chart that start with the letter 'd'.

In order to find the cities that end with the letter 'd', you would simply reverse the percentage sign and the letter in the format. It should look like the one shown below:

SELECT * FROM Clients
WHERE City LIKE '%d'

The results would bring up all of the clients that live in cities that end with the letter 'd'.

Let's say you wanted to find clients that lived in cities that had the word "land" in their name. You could use the format below in order to achieve your results:

SELECT * FROM Clients
WHERE City LIKE '%land%'

This would bring up clients that live in Portland, Orlando, and so on. By placing the percentage signs on the outside of the letters that you wish to find, you can make your search that much more specific to your needs.

Let's say you wanted to do the opposite of this specific search and you wanted to find clients that lived in cities that did not contain the word "land" in the name. You could do this by using the NOT keyword in the syntax shown below.

SELECT * FROM Clients
WHERE City NOT LIKE '%land%'

The result would bring up any clients that live in cities that do not contain the word "land" in their name.

NULL VALUES

As mentioned before, a null value will represent any missing or unknown data. As a result, a column can contain and hold null values. New data can be added or existing data can be updated without adding any value to the column if a column in a table is optional. You can do this by saving the field with a NULL VALUE. In tables, other values will be treated differently compared to null values. In order to use a placeholder for an unknown value or any value, NULL can be used. Keep in mind that NULL data and zero cannot be compared. They are not equivalent in these terms.

If you have a column that is considered option, the data can be saved with no value in this column. As a result, it will be saved with a NULL value instead of an actual value. The only way to test and know for sure if values in a chart is to use the operators IS NULL and IS NOT NULL.

In order to use the IS NULL operator:

SELECT Last,First,Address
FROM Clients
WHERE Address IS NULL

The result would bring up clients in your table that have columns of null value, or columns with no data. In this case, it would bring up clients that had no address entered into the database unless there happened to be any clients with missing first or last names.

In order to use the IS NOT NULL operator:

SELECT Last,First, Address
FROM Clients
WHERE Address IS NOT NULL

As a result, if what you searched before brought up clients that had no address entered into the database, this would bring up clients that did have addresses entered into the database. If there were any clients that had missing first or last name information for any reason, this would bring up any clients that had information filled out in all areas that were searched. This would bring up a list of clients with first and last names along with their address.

SELECT INTO

In order to select data from one table and insert it into another table, the SELECT INTO statement can be used. This can be useful when you need to attain backup copies of certain tables. This statement has the following formats:

In order to put all of the columns into a new table:

SELECT * INTO new_table_name
[IN externaldatabase]
FROM old_tablename

In order to select specific columns into a new table:

SELECT column_name(s)
INTO new_table_name
[IN externaldatabase]
FROM old_tablename

As mentioned, this can be useful when making backup copies of tables. Here are a few examples listed below:

In order to make an exact copy of data in the "Clients" table:

SELECT * INTO Clients_Backup
FROM Clients

In order to copy the table into another database, the IN clause can also be used:

SELECT * INTO Client_Backup
IN 'Backup.mdb'
FROM Clients

You can use the statement to only back up just a few fields to be copied into a new table:

SELECT Last,First
INTO Clients_Backup
FROM Clients

SELECT INTO with WHERE clause:

SELECT Last,First
INTO Clients_Backup
FROM Clients
WHERE City= 'Portland'

This would back up all clients that reside in the city of Portland.

SELECT INTO with joined tables:

SELECT Clients.Last,Orders.OrderNo
INTO Client_Order_Backup
FROM Clients
INNER JOIN Orders
ON Clients.C_Id=Orders.C_Id

The "Client_Order_Backup' table will result in containing data from the two tables of "Clients" and "Orders".

TOP

In order to specify the number of data that you want to be returned to you, the TOP clause can be used in order to achieve this. When working with many tables that need to be managed in a database, this can be a useful tool. Not all database systems will support the TOP clause though. It should be formatted as shown below:

SELECT TOP number | percent
column_name(s)
FROM table_name

There are two ways to use this clause in MySQL and Oracle:

MySQL:

SELECT column_name(s)
FROM table_name
LIMIT number

Oracle:

SELECT column_name(s)
FROM table_name
WHERE ROWNUM = number

TOP NUMBER:

For some examples, when you want to pull up only a certain number of clients in your table instead of the whole table, this can be done in the example shown below:

SELECT TOP 10 *
FROM Clients

The result would only bring up the top ten clients in a table instead of the whole table.

TOP PERCENT:

Let's say instead of focusing on a specific number, you wanted to focus on a percentage. In this case, you want to pull up the top 25% of clients in a table:

SELECT TOP 25 PERCENT *
FROM Clients

UNION

In order to combine two or more SELECT statements, the UNION clause can be used. The same number of columns must be the same as the ones specified in the SELECT statement when using the UNION clause. The same data types must also be involved as well. In each SELECT statement, the columns also need to be the same order. They should be formed as shown below:

SELECT column_name(s)
FROM table_name1
UNION
SELECT column_name(s)
FROM table_name2

By default, the UNION operator will only select distinct values. You can use the UNION ALL statement in order to allow duplicate values:

SELECT column_name(s)
FROM table_name1
UNION ALL
SELECT column_name(s)
FROM table_name2

In the first SELECT statement when using the UNION clause, the names of the columns will always be equal.

Let's say you want to bring up clients from two different cities. Let's say you want to pull up all the clients from Portland and Las Vegas:

SELECT Name
FROM Clients_Portland
UNION
SELECT Name
FROM Clients_LasVegas

The result will bring up clients in the database that live in those two specific cities. Although it seems like this would be the solution for bringing up all the clients listed in those two cities, it is not the case. This will only bring up the clients whose names are equal to each other. The

UNION command will only select distinct values.

In order to select all clients in two specific cities, use the UNION ALL formula shown below:

SELECT Name
FROM Clients_Portland
UNION ALL
SELECT Name
FROM Clients_LasVegas

This way, the only thing that changes compared to the previous formula is that the word "ALL" is added behind UNION and as a result, this brings up all the clients in those two specific cities.

VIEW

When using the VIEW command in SQL, it is based on the result-based table that will be shown on a virtual table. Just how a real table would appear, a view will contain rows and columns. The fields that are from one or more actual tables in the database are the fields that will appear in the VIEW function. Functions in SQL just like WHERE and JOIN can be used with the VIEW command in order to properly present the data.

CREATE VIEW:

CREATE VIEW view_name AS
SELECT column_name(s)
FROM table_name
WHERE condition

Keep in mind that a view will always show data in an up-to-date form. The database engine will recreate the data in order for it to appear in a view.

In order to update a VIEW:

CREATE OR REPLACE VIEW view_name AS
SELECT column_name(s)
FROM table_name
WHERE condition

In this example, the "Category" column will be added to the "Current Product List":

CREATE VIEW [Current Product List] AS
SELECT ProductID,ProductName,Category
FROM Products
WHERE Discontinued=No

The DROP VIEW command can be used in order to delete a view:

DROP VIEW view_name

WILDCARDS

In order to substitute one or more characters when searching data, wildcards can be useful for this purpose. A list of wildcards that can be used is listed below:

%- Can be used in order to substitute for zero or more characters.

_- Can be used in order to substitute for exactly one character.

[charlist]- Can be used in order to match a single character from a set of characters.

[^charlist] or **[!charlist]**- Can be used in order to match a single character that is not from a set of characters.

How to use the '%' Wildcard:

SELECT * FROM Clients WHERE City LIKE 'po%'

This would bring up cities that began with the letters, Po like, Portland.

This can also be used to look for a pattern. Just how it was mentioned in the "LIKE" command section, this wildcard can be used to pull up patterns in words. If you wanted to pull up the cities that had the word "land" in their name, you could do this with the example below:

SELECT * FROM Clients
WHERE City LIKE '%land%'

How to use the _ Wildcard:

This can be used in a way to pull up names of clients with specified letters in their name. Say you wanted to look up clients whose last name contained the letters "am". You could do this with the example below:

SELECT * FROM Clients
WHERE First LIKE '_am'

This would pull up names like "Campbell", "Cramer", or "Sampson".

Let's say you wanted to use this wildcard to replace certain letters in different places of a last name, you could do this with the example down below:

SELECT * FROM Clients
WHERE Last LIKE 'J_n_s'

This would pull up data like the last name "Jones".

How to use the [charlist] Wildcard:

SELECT * FROM Clients
WHERE Last LIKE '[cl]'

You could use this in order to pull up clients with last names that start with the letters c and l. You would pull up last names like Campbell and Lawson.

If you wanted to select clients with last names that did not start with c and l, you would use the formula shown below:

SELECT * FROM Clients
WHERE Last LIKE '[!cl]%'

You would not pull up last names like Campbell or Lawson. You would pull up last names like Anderson, Jones, or any last name that started with letters other than c or l.

Chapter 6:
Constraints in SQL

When you want to be able to limit what data can be entered into a table, you can make much use out of constraints. You can set up a constraint whenever a table is created. This can also be done by using the CREATE TABLE or ALTER TABLE commands. Listed below are some of the common constraints that can be used.

CHECK- This specifies a constraint that will limit the value range that can be placed in a column.

DEFAULT- This specifies a constraint that is used in order to insert a default value into a column.

FOREIGN KEY- This specifies a constraint that prevents invalid data from being inserted into the foreign key column because it has to be one of the values contained in the table that it points to.

NOT NULL- This specifies a constraint that enforces a column to not accept values that are null.

PRIMARY KEY- This specifies a constraint that uniquely identifies each record in a database table. It is important to note that each table should have a primary key and each table can only have one primary key.

UNIQUE- This specifies a constraint that uniquely identifies each record in a database table. It is important to note that a table can have many UNIQUE constraints, but only one PRIMARY KEY constraint.

CHECK

How to use the CHECK constraint on CREATE TABLE:

My SQL:

CREATE TABLE Clients
(C_Id int NOT NULL,
Last varchar (255) NOT NULL,
First varchar (255),
Address varchar (255),
City varchar (255),
CHECK (C_Id 0));

SQL Server/Oracle/Access:

CREATE TABLE Clients
(C_Id int NOT NULL
CHECK (C_Id 0),
Last varchar (255) NOT NULL,
First varchar (255),
Address varchar (255),
City varchar (255));

You can name and define a CHECK constraint on multiple columns:

MySQL/ SQL Server/ Oracle/ Access:

CREATE TABLE Clients
(C_Id int NOT NULL,
Last varchar (255) NOT NULL,
First varchar (255),
Address varchar (255),
City varchar (255),
CONSTRAINT chk_Client
CHECK (C_Id 0 AND City= 'LosAngeles'));

How to use the CHECK constraint on ALTER TABLE statement:

MySQL/ SQL Server/ Oracle/ Access:

ALTER TABLE Clients
ADD CHECK (C_Id 0)

MySQL/ SQL Server/ Oracle/ Access:

ALTER TABLE Clients
ADD CHECK (C_Id 0)

ALTER TABLE Clients
ADD CONSTRAINT chk_Clients
CHECK (C_Id 0 AND City= 'LasVegas')

How to DROP a CHECK constraint:

SQL Server/ Oracle/ Access:

ALTER TABLE Clients
DROP CONSTRAINT chk_Clients

DEFAULT

How to use the DEFAULT constraint with CREATE TABLE statement:

CREATE TABLE Clients
(Id int NOT NULL,
Last varchar (255) NOT NULL,
First varchar (255),
Address varchar (255),
City varchar (255)
DEFAULT 'LasVegas');

This will put a constraint on the "City" column when the "Clients" table is created. The DEFAULT constraint can even be used in order to insert system values by using functions such as GETDATE():

```
CREATE TABLE Orders
( ID int NOT NULL,
OrderNo int NOT NULL,
C_Id int,
OrderDate date
DEFAULT GETDATE());
```

How to use the DEFAULT constraint with ALTER TABLE statement:

MySQL:

```
ALTER TABLE Clients
ALTER City
SET DEFAULT 'LasVegas'
```

SQL Server/ Oracle/ Access:

```
ALTER TABLE Clients
ALTER COLUMN City
SET DEFAULT 'LasVegas'
```

How to DROP a DEFAULT constraint:

MySQL:

ALTER TABLE Clients
ALTER City DROP DEFAULT

SQL Server/ Oracle/ Access:

ALTER TABLE Clients
ALTER COLUMN City DROP DEFAULT

NOT NULL

This will enforce a column to not accept a null value. By default, a column is able to hold null values. In order to enforce a field to always contain a value, the NOT NULL constraint can be used. Without having to add a value to this field, you won't be able to enter new data.

How to use the NOT NULL constraint:

CREATE TABLE Clients
(C_Id int NOT NULL,
Last varchar (255) NOT NULL,
First varchar (255),
Address varchar (255),
City varchar (255));

PRIMARY KEY

In order to be able to uniquely identify each record in a database table, the PRIMARY KEY constraint can be used. A null value can't be held in a primary key column. A primary key should be in each table. Each table can only have one primary key.

How to use PRIMARY KEY on CREATE TABLE statement:

MySQL:

CREATE TABLE Clients
(C_Id int NOT NULL,
Last varchar (255) NOT NULL,
First varchar (255),
Address varchar (255),
City varchar (255),
PRIMARY KEY (C_Id));

SQL Server/ Oracle/ Access:

CREATE TABLE Clients
(C_Id int NOT NULL PRIMARY KEY,
Last varchar (255) NOT NULL,
First varchar (255),
Address varchar (255),
City varchar (255));

In order to name and define a PRIMARY KEY constraint on multiple   columns, use the following formula:

MySQL/ SQL Server/ Oracle/ Access:

CREATE TABLE Clients
(C_Id int NOT NULL,
Last varchar (255) NOT NULL,
First varchar (255),
Address varchar (255),
City varchar (255),
CONSTRAINT pk_PersonID PRIMARY
KEY (C_Id,Last));

How to use the PRIMARY KEY on ALTER TABLE statement:

MySQL/ SQL Server/ Oracle/ Access:

ALTER TABLE Clients
ADD PRIMARY KEY (C_Id)

Or the following can be used as well:

ALTER TABLE Clients
ADD CONSTRAINT pk_PersonID
PRIMARY KEY (C_Id,Last)

Keep in mind that when you use the ALTER TABLE statement that you also need to add a primary key. The columns must also already be declared to not be able to contain null values. This will be determined when the table is first created.

How to DROP a PRIMARY KEY constraint:

MySQL:

ALTER TABLE Clients
DROP PRIMARY KEY

SQL Server/ Oracle/ Access:

ALTER TABLE Clients
DROP CONSTRAINT pk_PersonID

FOREIGN KEY

The following statement will create a FOREIGN KEY on "C_Id" column when the "Orders" table is created.

How to use FOREIGN KEY with CREATE TABLE statement:

MySQL:

CREATE TABLE Orders
(O_Id int NOT NULL,
OrderNo int NOT NULL,
C_Id int,
PRIMARY KEY (O_Id),
FOREIGN KEY (C_Id) REFERENCES Clients
(C_Id))

SQL Server/ Oracle/ Access:

CREATE TABLE Orders
(O_Id int NOT NULL PRIMARY KEY
OrdersNo int NOT NULL,
C_Id int FOREIGN KEY REFERENCES Clients
(C_Id));

In order to name a FOREIGN KEY constraint and to define a FOREIGN KEY for multiple columns, use the following formula:

CREATE TABLE Orders
(O_Id int NOT NULL,
OrdersNo int NOT NULL,
C_Id int,
PRIMARY KEY (O_Id),
CONSTRAINT fk_PerOrders
FOREIGN KEY (C_Id)
REFERENCES Clients (C_Id));

How to use the FOREIGN KEY with the ALTER TABLE statement:

ALTER TABLE Orders
ADD FOREIGN KEY (C_Id)
REFERENCES Clients (C_Id)

This will create a FOREIGN KEY constraint on the "C_Id" column when the "Orders" table is already created.

ALTER TABLE Orders
ADD CONSTRAINT fk_PerOrders
FOREIGN KEY (C_Id)
REFERENCES Clients (C_Id)

This will name a FOREIGN KEY constraint and to define it also on multiple columns.

How to DROP a FOREIGN KEY constraint:

MySQL:

ALTER TABLE Orders
DROP FOREIGN KEY fk_PerOrders

SQL Server/ Oracle/ Access:

ALTER TABLE Orders
DROP CONSTRAINT fk_PerOrders

UNIQUE

The UNIQUE constraint can be used to identify each record uniquely in a database. The UNIQUE and PRIMARY KEY constraints will both provide a certain amount of uniqueness for a set of columns or a column by itself. A PRIMARY KEY constraint will automatically have a UNIQUE constraint defined on it.

How to use the UNIQUE constraint on the CREATE TABLE statement:

MySQL:

CREATE TABLE Clients
(C_Id int NOT NULL,
Last varchar (255) NOT NULL,
First varchar (255),
Address varchar (255),
City varchar (255),
UNIQUE (C_Id));

SQL Server/ Oracle/ Access:

CREATE TABLE Clients
(C_Id int NOT NULL UNIQUE,
Last varchar (255) NOT NULL,
First varchar (255),
Address varchar (255),
City varchar (255));

In order to name a UNIQUE constraint and to define a UNIQUE constraint on multiple columns:

CREATE TABLE Clients
(C_Id int NOT NULL,
Last varchar (255) NOT NULL,
First varchar (255),
Address varchar (255),
City varchar (255),
CONSTRAINT uc_PersonID
UNIQUE (C_Id,Last));

How to use the UNIQUE constraint on ALTER TABLE:

ALTER TABLE Clients
ADD UNIQUE (C_Id)

This is in order to create a UNIQUE constraint on the "C_Id" column when the table has already been created.

In order to name a UNIQUE constraint and in order to define a UNIQUE constraint on multiple columns use the following formula below:

ALTER TABLE Clients
ADD CONSTRAINT uc_PersonID
UNIQUE (C_Id,Last)

In order to DROP a UNIQUE constraint:

MySQL:

ALTER TABLE Clients
DROP INDEX uc_PersonID

SQL Server/ Oracle/ Access:

ALTER TABLE Clients
DROP CONSTRAINT uc_PersonID

Chapter 7:
SQL Joins and Functions

JOINS

In order to query data from two or more tables that are based on a relationship between certain columns in tables, the JOIN keyword can be used in an SQL statement. Keys allow tables in databases to be related to each other. Below is a list of the types of JOINS found in SQL.

INNER JOIN- This will return rows when there is at least one match found in both tables.

LEFT JOIN- This will return all the rows from the left table, even if there are no matches in the right table.

RIGHT JOIN- This will return all the rows from the right side of the table, even if there are no matches in the left table.

FULL JOIN- This will return the rows when there is a match in one of the tables.

FULL JOIN

SELECT column_name(s)
FROM table_name1
FULL JOIN table_name2
ON
table_name1.column_name=table_name2.colu
mn_name

INNER JOIN

SELECT column_name(s)
FROM table_name1
INNER JOIN table_name2
ON
table_name1.column_name=table_name2.colu
mn_name

It is important to note that an INNER JOIN is the same as the JOIN keyword.

LEFT JOIN

SELECT column_name(s)
FROM table_name1
LEFT JOIN table_name2
ON
table_name1.column_name=table_name2.colu
mn_name

RIGHT JOIN

SELECT column_name(s)
FROM table_name1
RIGHT JOIN table_name2
ON
table_name1.column_name=table_name2.colu
mn_name

FUNCTIONS

Some of these functions have been mentioned earlier in this book. Here, we will go over some of them and how to put them to use in a database. Listed below are some main functions:

Aggregate Functions

These types of functions will return a single value that is calculated from values in a column.

AVG()- This will return the average value.

COUNT()- This will return the number of rows.

FIRST()- This will return the first value.

LAST()- This will return the last value.

MAX()- This will return the largest value.

MIN()- This will return the smallest value.

SUM()- This will return the sum.

Scalar Functions

These types of functions will return a single value based on the input value.

UCASE()- This will convert a field to upper case.

LCASE()- This will convert a field to lower case.

MID()- This will extract characters from a text field.

LEN()- This will return the length of a text field.

ROUND()- This will round a numeric field to the number of decimals specified.

NOW()- This will return the current system date and time.

FORMAT()- This will format how a field is to be displayed.

AVG()

SELECT AVG (column_name)
FROM table_name

An example of how you could use this more accurately in a table is if you have a list of prices for product held.

SELECT AVG (Price) AS Average
FROM Orders

COUNT()

SELECT COUNT (column_name)
FROM table_name

COUNT(*)

This function will return the number of records in a table.

SELECT COUNT (*)
FROM table_name
COUNT (DISTINCT column_name)

SELECT COUNT (DISTINCT column_name)
FROM table_name

Keep in mind that this function will not work in Access.

FIRST()

SELECT FIRST (column_name)
FROM table_name

Here is an example of how the function works:

SELECT FIRST (Price) AS FirstPrice
FROM Orders

FORMAT()

SELECT FORMAT (column_name, format)
FROM table_name

Here is an example of how to use this function when applying a date format:

SELECT Product, Price,
FORMAT(Now(), 'YYYY-MM-DD') AS CurDate
FROM Products

This would add a column in a table that contains the current date.

LAST()

SELECT LAST (column_name)
FROM table_name

Here is an example of how this function would be used:

SELECT LAST (Price) AS LastPrice
FROM Orders

LCASE()/ LOWER()

Here are the two ways that this function can be formatted:

SELECT LCASE(column_name)
FROM table_name
SELECT LOWER(column_name)
FROM table_name

Here is an example of how this function would be put to use:

SELECT LCASE(Last) AS Last,First
FROM Clients

LEN()

SELECT LEN(column_name)
FROM table_name

Here is an example of how the function would be put to use:

SELECT LEN(City) AS LengthOfCity
FROM Clients

MAX()

SELECT MAX(column_name)
FROM table_name

Here is an example of the function:

SELECT MAX(Price) AS LargestPrice
FROM Orders

MID()

SELECT MID(column_name,start,[length])
FROM table_name

Here is an example of the function:

SELECT MID(City,1,3) AS CityShort
FROM Clients

MIN()

SELECT MIN(column_name)
FROM table_name

Here is an example of how the function:

SELECT MIN(Price) AS SmallestPrice
FROM Orders

NOW()

SELECT NOW ()
FROM table_name

Here is an example of the function:

SELECT Product, Price, Now() AS CurDate
FROM Products

ROUND()

SELECT   ROUND(column_name,decimals)
FROM table_name

Here is an example of the function:

SELECT Product, ROUND(Price,0) AS Price
FROM Products

SUM()

SELECT SUM(column_name)
FROM table_name

Here is an example of the function:

SELECT SUM(Price) AS Total
FROM Orders

UCASE()/ UPPER()

There are two ways that this function can be formed:

SELECT UCASE(column_name)
FROM table_name

SELECT UPPER(column_name)
FROM table_name

Here is an example of the function:

SELECT UCASE(Last) AS Last,First
FROM Clients

Types of SQL Comments

Comments will be used in order to clarify the purpose of SQL statements. Here are a couple of the comment types and the ways that they can be included within an SQL statement:

Line Comments

These types of comments are indicated by the presence of two hyphens (--). The text left after these hyphens will be the comment.

It should look like: -- with the line comment here

Block Comments

These types of comments will be indicated by the presence of /* which will be the beginning of the comment and the end of the comment will be indicated by */. This kind of comment can cover part of the text that is in a line, or it can span multiple lines.

It will look like:

/* block comment placed here */

Chapter 8:
Other Useful Terms

Character Data Types

- Char(n)- This is for storing a fixed-length character string. The maximum length is 8,000 characters.

- Varchar(n)- This is for storing a variable-length character string. The maximum length is 8,000 characters.

- Varchar(max)- This is for storing a variable-length character string. The maximum length is 1,073,741,824 characters.

- Text- This is for storing a variable-length character string. The maximum amount is 2 GB of data in text.

Unicode Strings

- Nchar(n)- This is for storing fixed-length unicode data. The maximum length is 4,000 characters.

- Nvarchar(n)- This is for storing variable-length unicode data. The maximum length is 4,000 characters.

- Nvarchar(max)- This is for storing variable-length unicode data. The maximum length is 536,870,912 characters.

- Ntext- This is for storing variable-length unicode data. The maximum amount is 2 GB of text data.

Binary Data Types

- Bit- This allows 0, 1, or NULL.

- Binary(n)- This is for storing fixed-length binary data. The maximum is 8,000 bytes.

- Varbinary(n)- This is for storing variable-length binary data. The maximum is 8,000 bytes.

- Varbinary(max)- This is for storing variable-length binary data. The maximum is 2 GB.

- Image- This is for storing variable length binary data. The maximum is 2 GB.

Numeric Data Types

- Tinyint- This allows 0 to 255 numbers to be stored. The storage is 1 byte.

- Smallint- This allows numbers to be stored between -32,768 and 32,767. The storage is 2 bytes.

- Int- This allows whole numbers between -2,147,483,648 and 2,147,483,647. The storage is 4 bytes.

- Bigint- This allows numbers between -9,223,372,036,854,775,808 and 9,223,372,036,854,775,807 to be stored. The storage is 8 bytes.

- Decimal(p,s)- This is for storing fixed precision and scale numbers. It allows numbers from $-10^{38} +1$ to $10^{38} -1$ to be stored. The p parameter will indicate the digits of maximum amount that can be stored in total. This contains both numbers to the right and left of a decimal point. A value between 1 and 38 should be assigned for the p parameter. The default is 18. Th maximum amount of digits and how many can be stored to the right of the decimal point will be indicated by the s parameter. The s must be of a value of 0 to the p. 0 is the default. The storage is 5-17 bytes.

- Numeric(p,s)- This is for fixed precision and scale numbers. It allows numbers between -10^38 +1 to 10^38 - 1. The p parameter will indicate the maximum number of digits that can be stored in total. This contains both the numbers left and right of the decimal point. The p must be a value between 1 and 38. The default is 18. The s parameter will indicate the amount of digits to be stored to the right of the decimal point. The s must be a value of 0 to the p. The default is 0. The storage is 5-17 bytes.

- Smallmoney- This is for storing monetary data between -214,748.3648 to 214,748.3647. The storage is 4 bytes.

- Money- This is for storing monetary data between -922,337,203,685,477.5808 to 922,337,203,685,477.5807. The storage is 8 bytes.

- Float(n)- This is for storing a floating precision number from -1.79E + 308 to 1.79E + 308. Whether the field should hold either 4 or 8 bytes will be indicated by the n parameter. Float (24) holds a field of 4 bytes while float(53) holds a field of 8 bytes. 53 is the default value of the n parameter. The storage will be between 4 and 8 bytes.

- Real- This is for storing a number of floating precision between -3.40E + 38 and 3.40E + 38. The storage is 4 bytes.

Date/Time Data Types

- Datetime- This is for storing a date anywhere between January 1, 1753, and December 31, 9999. This has an accuracy of 3.33 milliseconds. The storage is 8 bytes.

- Datetime2- This is in order to store a date anywhere between January 1, 0001 and December 31, 9999. 100 nanoseconds is its accuracy. The storage is 6 to 8 bytes.

- Smalldatetime- This is in order to store a date anywhere between January 1, 1900, and June 6, 2079. One minute is its accuracy. The storage is 4 bytes.

- Date- This is for storing only a date. Any date between January 1, 0001 to December 31, 9999. The storage is 3 bytes.

- Time- This is for storing only time. 100 nanoseconds is its accuracy. The storage is between 3 to 5 bytes.

- Datetimeoffset- With the addition of a time zone offset, datetime2 is the same thing. The storage is between 8 and 10 bytes.

- Timestamp- Every time that a row is either created or modified, this will store a unique number. The timestamp is based on an internal clock and won't correspond with real time. Each table may only have one timestamp variable.

Conclusion

Although SQL may be thought of as a complicated subject, it actually can be quite easy to learn and comprehend when broken down and put to practice. No matter what your reasons are for learning this useful skill, it can highly benefit you in the business world and open up doors for you later on in your career path. Although there are complicated processes and terms involved with SQL, learning how to break them down into ideas that you can understand makes it all worth it.

By putting the use of SQL into practice, you will only be able to further understand how this language works with other databases. Take time to practice what you learn and go at your own pace. The commands, operators, clauses and keywords are here for your own use whenever you are stumped or when you forget how a syntax should be formed. Make use of this book as you make your way into your skill of SQL.

Start out with the simpler steps before moving on to the more complicated ones. Only move on to the more advanced steps when you feel up to the challenge or you want to try out something on your own. You may surprise yourself when you realize how simple SQL can be.

Although this has been written with examples of clients or inventory charts, there are many uses for databases. The examples given are not to be taken completely literal. You can use the information in this book to fit whatever your needs are for any database.

Remember to keep an open mind when moving forward and you will keep any issues from becoming more complicated than what they need to be. As mentioned, SQL can be a simple thing to learn. You just need to take the time to understand what everything fully means in depth. If something doesn't turn out as expected, retrace your tracks to find where you might have inappropriately added a formula and some of the information. By building and maintaining successful problem-solving skills, you will have no limit to your success and to your potential for enhanced performance. Open doors for your future or present career by making good use of your newly acquired skills in SQL. Also, remember to never stop trying to learn all that is offered in SQL. Continuing your education in order to even better understand SQL is always worth the time and energy that you put into yourself, your career, and even your business.

Additionally, please visit our Amazon Author page for more great info and resources.

https://www.amazon.com/Mark-Anderson/e/B01N51MTHL

You will find all the books you need to learn about:

Python Programming, SQL, JavaScript, and even **TOR** if that's something you fancy!!

https://www.amazon.com/HACKING-Beginner-Penetration-Security-Programming-ebook/dp/B01N8ZF5F4

https://www.amazon.com/PYTHON-Beginner-Practical-Programming-Beginners-ebook/dp/B01N91WKHD

Last but not least, if you enjoyed this book and thought it was helpful, we certainly won't say no to a 5-star **review on Amazon**.

Thank You and Best of Luck in Your SQL Programming Endeavors!!!